Arelhe-kenhe Merrethene

Arrernte Traditional Healing

Arelhe-kenhe Merrethene

Arrernte Traditional Healing

compiled by
Veronica Perrurle Dobson

IAD PRESS

Published by IAD Press 2007
PO Box 2531
Alice Springs NT 0871
Tel: 08 8951 1334
Fax: 08 8951 1381
Email: sales@iad.edu.au
www.iad.edu.au/press

National Library of Australia
Cataloguing-in-Publication data:

Dobson, Veronica (Veronica Perrurle).
Arelhe-kenhe Merrethene : Arrernte traditional healing.

Includes index.
ISBN 978 1 86465 033 4

1. Aboriginal Australian healers – Australia. 2. Aranda
(Australian people) – Northern Territory – Alice Springs
Region – Medicine. 3. Aboriginal Australians – Northern
Territory –Alice Springs Region – Health and hygiene. I.
Title.

615.88089915

Cover: Darren Pfitzner
Design and layout: Lynn Twelftree Art & Design
Map: Shann Twelftree
Printed in Australia by Hyde Park Press

Australian Government

Australia Council
for the Arts

The Institute for Aboriginal Development
Incorporated is assisted by the Australian
Government through the Australia Council,
its arts funding and advisory body.

DEDICATION

*this book is dedicated to the healers from
the past that used this type of healing*

Angangkere ilyernpenye

Arelhe nhenhe rlkerte anthurre, tyerrtye arrpenhe nhenhe mape angkerreme-le aneme.

"Anwerne akweye angangkere inetyeke alheye."

Arelhe rlkerte nhenhe renhe aretyeke apetyetyeke, iwenhe-le renhe rlkerte ileke. Nhakwe angangkere atherre aneme apwerte artepenye ikngerre nhakwe-le.

Renhe atherrenhe ikngwetye-ke mpwele alherraye, nhenhe renhe aretye-ke apetyetye-ke mwerre apeke ilemele. Kele angangkere re atherre arratye apetyeke rlkerte mwerre ilemele mpware-ke awelye-le arlke ilyeme-le. Re anteme angkwe inteke angangkere le mpware-ke iperre, angkwe inteke iperre rlkerte re akemirreme-le mwerre ulkere anteme awelheme.

Angangkere anwerne-kenhe ilyernpenye anthurre aneke. Rlkerte anwerne kenhe arntarnte areme-le. Kele.

This woman is very sick, some of these people are sitting around talking. "We will have to go and get a healer to come and see the sick woman, what is making her sick. The two healers live at the back of that hill towards the east that way."

"Let's go and get them to come, come on. Let's go, so that they can come and see what's wrong with her and maybe make her well again, sing her with the healing song so that she could sleep after the healers have cured her."

After sleeping it off she will get up feeling a lot better. Our healers were very clever in those days, looking after our sick.

Angangkere ilyernpenye

Tyepetye is a traditional Arrernte story-telling practice. Women use leaves to represent the characters in a story, and they draw lines in the sand to represent windbreaks, fires and other parts of the story as the action unfolds.

Here, the story-teller smooths the sand before starting to tell the story. She uses the leaves of the *utyerrke* and some twigs, and a *mane-mane*, a story-telling stick.

Angangkere ilyernpenye

Moving the leaves that represent the healers and the messenger, the story-teller shows the journey they took to reach the sick person.

Three people sitting near a fire talk about the sick person.

People gather around the healers while they are helping the sick person.

After the healing has been done, the healers and the messenger leave.

CONTENTS

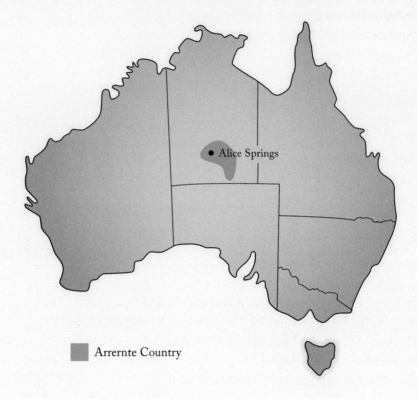

Arrernte Country

ACKNOWLEDGMENTS

Many people have contributed to the spiritual healing and traditional medicine project. It's not possible to give more than basic information about each person's contribution.

Researched and compiled by Veronica Dobson

Main Arrernte Contributors:
   Douglas Wallace Peltharre (dec)
   Philomena Maggie Young Peltharre
   Basil Hayes Perrurle
   Veronica Dobson Perrurle
   Basil Stevens Peltharre (dec)
   Davey Hayes Angale (dec)

Other written material was provided by the *Eastern and Central Arrernte Dictionary* and *Bushfires and Bushtucker*. IAD has supported and administered the funding for this work to be completed. Other bodies have given funding for this project: the main research has been funded by the Australian Institute of Aboriginal and Torres Strait Islander Studies (AIATSIS), and other financial support came from the University of Western Australia. Thanks also go to John Henderson, Jeannie Devitt, Jenny Green, Patrick McConvell, Barry McDonald and Margaret McDonell.

Eastern and Central Arrernte Dictionary, compiled by John Henderson and Veronica Dobson, IAD Press, Alice Springs, 1994

Bushfires and Bushtucker: Aboriginal Plant Use in Central Australia, Peter Latz, IAD Press, Alice Springs, 1995

INTRODUCTION

I was born out at Arltunga, but I count myself as belonging to *Ltyentye Apurte* (Sanat Teresa). I follow my grandfather's footprints (my father's father) there. I relate to his country in the same way as I do to my grandfather himself. I'm belonging to that country, Ltyentye Apurte. My other grandfather, my mother's father, worked at Ross River, at Atnape station, and also at Undoolya station. We lived at Ross River when I was a child and my grandfather told us that we had to go back to the Catholic Mission out at Arltunga and attend school there.

Then he took us back to the Mission near where the goldmine was happening. That's where we started going to school. I was only small when they took me into the dormitory, I was five years old. We lived out at Arltunga attending school there and we learnt a lot. After a while the Mission shifted from Arltunga to Santa Teresa because the drinking water was no good. After the miners washed the gold with cyanide they let the water spill into the river, and our people used water from soaks for drinking. The water tasted bitter because of the poison.

When we lived out at Santa Teresa, we were taught in English when we were still only small children. You know, when you are only a small child just speaking your mother tongue, you don't know – and wonder – what the European person expects of you. This is what we thought when we spoke in our own language. They used to tell us off – 'Don't talk that yabba-yabba language. We want to teach you in English.' That is what they used to tell us – when we spoke in Arrernte they'll tell us off. We used to wonder why we weren't allowed to speak our language. We were made to learn in their language. Well, when we got older we could see why they were trying to teach us in the English language. After leaving school we were put into the workforce, learning to do domestic work like ironing, house cleaning, working in the laundry and cooking. They taught us about how to live clean, and if we didn't know English we wouldn't have been able to work and live like this. I'm glad that I learned English, because now I have two languages, and now I'm able to write this book. I wrote it in my own language, Arrernte, first and then translated it into English.

Our people always used to use these traditional medicines, see. When we went back down to the camp during school holidays for two or three weeks, our families would take us out bush and sit down with us using traditional medicines and also collecting and eating lots of bush foods.

I have wanted to write about this, like other people do. There might be Europeans and other Aboriginal people that want to write about traditional medicines as well. I've made something about the traditional medicines in this book, also about the healing fat and how the elders used it to cure their sick. I worked on that. I went along with a tape recorder and asked people for some information on traditional medicine and the healing fat. They told me the story about how the elders used these medicines in the early days, and how if you got sick from something that may have been done to you, the healer would help make you well again. These are the things that I asked them about.

They told me how they used to heal and cure their sick after being boned, or if they got bad 'flus. These are my families, and people from this area are still family to me. I've learnt from my families and from our elders, from my grandmothers (father's mother and mother's mother), also my grandfathers (father's father and mother's father). They used to do that old healing when people got sick, singing them with the healing song and rubbing the fat onto the body, whether it's an adult or a child that got the 'flu and gets hot and cold fevers. Healing songs are sung over the sick and the healing fat is then rubbed onto the person, helping them heal and get well.

The olden days

In the early days in this big wide open country, there was always healing cures here on the Land – the healing songs, fat, paintings and the healers – and it's still the same now, even after all the old-time elders have passed on. The Land still has that power. The healing belongs to the country where it originated from, and belongs to the people from that country. The healing fat, the song and the painting, they all originated at a particular place and that's where they all belong. Each different Arrernte country – and there are lots of them – has their own healing fat, songs and paintings.

If someone is going to be a healer, the elders choose who it's going to be. The elders see who had the special gift, and they are the people that are chosen to become healers. The chosen person is then put to sleep and taken through their country that they relate to. The elders then teach the chosen one about the healing, taking them through with the *Irrernte-arenye* (little spirit people). That's how it was done in the early days, and it still happens, but it has changed a bit. The healing comes from lots of things like the goanna, emu, wasp, kangaroo and others. The *awelye* healing song is sung from the country. We still remember about the healing from our elders. However, some of the other ideas from our elders, the younger generation has forgotten about now. They make their own bodies sick and unwell by drinking alcohol and eating fatty foods and modern meat.

Aboriginal people's living standards changed after the Europeans came. The kidney, liver, and high blood pressure affected Aboriginal people who ate lots of sweets. Children eat too many of these types of food and they don't eat many bush foods. Only Europeans' medicines can cure those things. Our healers are unable to cure these types of illnesses.

In the early days in Alice Springs and surrounding cattle stations, Arrernte people didn't drink too much alcohol – that's why people never got sick much. They used to only buy a little bit of food to add to what they got from the bush, and they looked after themselves, and the families all stayed together, not doing anything wrong. All the people lived in their skin system groups without saying or doing anything wrong to anyone else. They all lived in harmony. They ate lots of good foods and meat from the bush, and a lot of people in the early days used to walk around on foot. People that lived in the town area and from Middle Park used to always walk into the township – never drove – and also they used to walk into the hills looking for witchetty grubs and other bush foods. People were happy just drinking water from the soakages, water from the country, because the water from the country they know belongs to them – it's part of them, and that is how we think.

Other peoples' country was always respected – that's how it used to be. It's true that today some people's kidney gets sick because they drink too much alcohol, and get sick from the naked mangy dogs that they live with. People now don't look after themselves. The children are always being fed takeaway foods, takeaway all the time and no food that has been cooked at home – foods the elders cooked, like dampers and stews.

In those early days the people looked after their children, the young girls at least listened to what their elders told them – well, there's no more listening now. It's not like that any more. That's why things go wrong for people now, getting all these sicknesses. In the early days people were left to die, nowadays they are kept alive by machines. For some families it's hard to donate someone a kidney. It would be good to talk to people that have donated their kidney to someone, and find out what they think when they donate a kidney to someone in the family. Do you know that the person will be good after you donate your kidney to them? It's part of you that you're giving to them, the person you donate the kidney to is one of you, that person is part of you too. They should look after themselves and not start to drink again.

Our people in the early days killed *aherre* (kangaroos), *arenge* (euros), they killed for meat only what they really needed. The skins of these animals were eaten too, and nothing was wasted. The skins were peeled off and placed on top of the *ilthe* (humpy) or on an *amamere* (a type of tree platform). They were laid out to dry and stored with other foods covered with brush leaves. When people couldn't get meat to eat, the dried skin was cooked and softened in the hot sand and ash, then pounded with a rock to make it rip off easily and that's how it was eaten, that's how it was. It was the elders who used to eat the skins, never the children. The animals that were eaten, and other bush foods, were respected and looked after. People only picked and killed what they could eat.

Our people in the early days used to do lots of things. Have their ceremonies, men's ceremonies and other celebrations while on walkabout around the country. Look after the sacred sites, hunt *kere* (meat animals), touch up the cave paintings, make artefacts. People of today don't do these things too much. The paintings in the caves are pretty dull now. Our elders always used to look after the carvings in the caves. They kept the caves and the country clean. Women did their ceremonies too, all around their countries. They may go for weeks on ceremony business. If the country was looking good they'd stay there for a while. That's how the elders lived in the early days.

The older women used to take the young girls and teach them about the animal meats and bush foods while going walkabout, showing them the country, telling them how they relate to country and through whom: 'This is the *atyunpe* (perentie), this is the *arlewatyerre* (goanna)', or whatever other animals that's used for meat. They can learn about how they are cooked and to treat all foods, meats and vegetables, with respect. 'The banana vine, the flowers, bush onions – do not use a stick to dig them with.' 'The roots of the bush banana – after digging, cover the hole.' That's how our elders taught their young women.

A group of Arrernte people camping near the site of the Telegraph Station at Alice Springs, showing a windbreak and traditional *ilthe* (humpy), made of *irreye* (old man saltbush), May 1923.
Photo Baldwin Spencer, reproduced courtesy of Museum Victoria

Medicine was collected and made up to use, plant medicine especially was used regularly, while they lived on the Land. Whatever they did, they did well. The older men went walkabout, teaching young men about hunting. The young men went along and learned about country.

Our elders in the early days lived in harmony, with their spirits and country intact, and with no serious sickness. When people of the country go back to their Land even today, their bodies start to feel better and they feel good about themselves.

That's what the elders used to say – the wide open country is the healer, and that the healing song, the painting, they are all intact there, they all created there together. We remember that very clearly. When we were children we used to see what the elders did when they approached a place after travelling. They would start singing – they always started singing. Even when they walked around on the country, they would sing their healing song on their country. The elders from the early days knew and remembered this always, and we still remember this too, because they always used to tell us about it. Even nowadays, when someone goes back to country after being away for a long time living somewhere else, their homeland makes them feel good about themselves, and makes them know who they are and where they belong. The Land heals them.

When you return after being away for a while, the country you're returning to seems to get further away from you, as if you're a stranger. But you long to get there because the country's welcoming you at the same time, knowing that you are coming home and that you belong there. That's the feeling you get – that's how traditional people see it. Because you've been away from your country for too long, the country desires to further itself from you, making you suffer a bit. The person thinks the country is further, making them really long for it. 'When are we ever going to get there? Why is it this far away?' After being away for too long you feel bad about it. But the country from where you originated takes you back, making you feel well and good about yourself. It's almost as though the country gets brighter and more colourful, more alive – happy to have you back. That's what's good about this country of ours.

Some countries are really strong. When a stranger who is not from the country goes to places like *Anthwerrke* (Emily Gap), they may feel no good. Maybe if they swim in the water something bad might happen. Like someone drowning, if they enter into the water at a strange place. It's alright for people from those areas themselves to swim in the waters, but strangers should really take care when they enter other people's country because the country plays tricks on them. Most places have spiritual connections to our Ancestors and they play certain tricks on strangers, making them sick. That's why people's hair stands on end when they go to places like *Anthwerrke*,

Akapulye (Jessie Gap) or wherever. The spirits of our Ancestors and the little spirit people – they belong there, and they are watching you all carefully. If you are not from there, the little spirit people of the country can make you deluded by making you lose your mind, and the country looks different, causing you to feel sick. If you are a stranger to the country, that's what happens to you – that's just how it is.

When people from *Anthwerrke* and *Akapulye* areas go to these places they speak to their Ancestor spirits by picking up handfuls of sand and throwing the sand around, saying, 'It's me and the family – we are coming home', singing out, telling the spirits – 'it's me, my Ancestors'. After doing that, you can stay or walk around at these places. That's how we are now even still, always when going back to country – letting the Ancestor spirits know we have come home to country and to them.

Sacred sites or Dreaming sites are places that are of importance to our people. Places like *Anthwerrke*, *Akapulye*. When the old people were alive, they lined up behind one another, walking on one another's footprints. That's how people walked around in these areas, out of respect for the country. These sites can make you feel unwelcome, make you get a headache and make you feel unwell. If the place doesn't recognize you, that is when it makes you sick, by making your head ache.

It was like this in the olden days, and our healers were very special to us all. There's only a handful of good healers around now. The healing power gets lost, we believe that, with the seriousness of alcohol, the power of healing gets frightened away and leaves.

OVERLEAF: *Mpwaltye* (Honeymoon Gap)

Spiritual healing

Utnenge – Spirit

Everybody has a spirit – big people, little children. Every living thing
has a spirit. The spirit is an important part of your body. When
something dies the spirit leaves it and goes – the body is no longer
alive. The spirit is an important part of everybody's life – that's what
keeps you alive. When people get sick as a result of boning, their
spirit gets weak and tired, and sickness results, the body gets sick.
When a person gets a fright while sleeping, their spirit leaves them,
and the person gets sick also.

Then you have to call the healer to come and cure the sick
person with his hands. The healer cures the sick person by getting
the sick person's spirit and placing it back into their body, making
them well again. A child loses their spirit when someone frightens
them when they are sleeping. It's the same for an adult, especially
older people. When you frighten them while they are asleep, they get

sick and their spirit leaves the body. The spirit is very special. Don't talk too loud, or you will frighten someone that is asleep and make them sick, and only the traditional healer can cure this. That is the way our elders did their healing and others are still doing this today.

It is the Aboriginal way to put and use curses on people. That is one of the reasons why people's spirits leave them. Also, people should stay on their own country. People that come from other country, their spirit leaves them and goes, and then the person gets sick. Lots of children get sick because they grow up without their spirits, if their parents have moved away from their homeland. Some people will always have their spirits disappear when they get a fright or scared of something. But other people, like when they get scared from dogs – that's because their spirits are not in the proper place. Families' spirits are not in the proper place anymore. When a child's spirit doesn't settle, then it makes their families unhappy, because it's not their country they're living on, and they may want to go back to their own country. People who are not on their own country are also at risk from being cursed by other people or by the Land itself.

Angangkere – Traditional healers

The power of healing comes from the country of whoever is chosen to become a healer. The elders of the tribe chose the rightful people to be healers. Traditional country is where the healing power comes from, waiting to hand down the power to the ones who are becoming healers. Handing down the healing songs and the healing fat, everything like that.

The power of the healer comes from the country where they originated. Just like when people go back to country they feel better, the country has the power to heal and cleanse. The traditional healers get their power to cure sick people from the Land and its spirits. Power was given to them from our Ancestor spirits to cure illnesses and the effects from boning. Only certain people can become traditional healers. The chosen person is put into a deep sleep, and then his or her mind and spirit travel with the little spirit people and with our Ancestor spirits, through the country. They learn about healing songs, and how to heal by touch, and about the *awelye* for the country. Our Ancestors sing with the little spirit people, while giving the knowledge and the power to whoever is becoming the new traditional healer. That is how our Ancestors did it with the people who were chosen to become healers. That is how it's still getting done now with a few changes, much like our Ancestors have done it all along.

The traditional healers are supposed to travel with the little spirit people, that's what I was told. They learn about the powers of the Land, and about what the Land has to offer. The older healers travel as real people, in their bodies, with the little spirit people, but it's only the spirit of the person who is being taught to become a healer that travels with them. The stories, the songs, the healing and the Dreaming are all seen by the learner as if in a dream, as if they were asleep while it is all happening. As if in a dream − that is how the healer makes the learner feel, by putting them to sleep, making their spirit and mind travel through their rightful country, wherever it is, like it was a really long journey. There is where they will see all they have learned, now that they themselves are a healer. They return as one of the healers, after letting their spirit and mind travel in the country they're related to and that has given them the power as a healer. They live and die still as a healer. As they get older they give their healing powers to others who are in line, and that have been chosen to receive the power of healing.

The knowledge is given to these people on their own country. The little spirit people, and the older healers, they both have Dreamings or totems from that country, and they continue to use their healing powers and songs. They still follow their customs, while passing on to the younger healers the traditional knowledge.

The traditional healer gets his power from the country to which he is related. Some people are children when that happens. The older healer sees the special gift the person has. That's how it happens for whoever the elders choose to be healers. Today, some people keep this knowledge and these customs and laws like the elders did – they follow in their footsteps.

Before you become a traditional healer you go through the Law of the little spirit people, and through the Land that the Dreaming of the healing power comes from, to your *Altyerre Aknganentye* or totem and country.

When they travel in their spirit, the new healers learn about the healing songs and how to use their hands to heal with, and how to apply the healing fat onto the sick person to make them well. Then, when other people get sick, these younger healers can cleanse them, making them well again. They have learned how to heal with their hands, how to sing the healing songs for someone. The person that has just become a healer is carefully watched, making sure that they use the proper methods to heal with.

The healer uses the healing song to sing the fat, then the fat is rubbed onto the person's body. The person himself is also sung with the healing song while the fat is being rubbed on. The songs come from the Dreaming, and could be about *arntinye* (wasps), *arleye* (emus), perenties, kangaroos, *inarlenge* (porcupines), goannas and *Arrwekelenye-areye* (other Ancestors).

Arratye anthurre – this type of healing was used by our Ancestors

Alharrkentye (Trephina Gorge)

and it's still being practised today. The healing powers have been handed down from generation to generation to the rightful people who are chosen to be healers. The Law relating to the healing power hasn't changed for our people over the years – it still stays the same.

You know how we believe in God? Well, the traditional healer is a special person like that. That's how we see it. When people get sick, the healer is there to cure them, cleansing them of the illness. Our Ancestors left all their knowledge behind for us to use when they returned to their resting places, so that it can be handed down to the younger people. After the young ones learn, they keep handing the knowledge down to *their* children. The healer is a special person in peoples' lives. When there weren't any European people around, our healers did all the healing of their own people, singing them with the healing songs of the country. Whatever different connection it has to the place – the healing song might be from the *irlkngerre-irlkngerre* (cricket), emu, goanna, or other things that may belong to the healer's country – the healers always use their hands to cure while applying the sung healing fat onto people. They also sometimes heal by touching the head. Some traditional healers heal just by touching someone who is ill. These healers of ours are very clever, without them we would have all died from catching other diseases.

Sometimes another traditional healer might make you sick with his power. He then has to cure you himself. Because he's got the power that made you sick in the first place, he's got to make you well again. Then he sings, heals you with his hands, and makes you well, fit and strong again. That's how the traditional healers did their healing in the early days for people that may have been made sick by their own power, whether a child or an adult. You go to another healer and they will tell you, 'Go to the one that made you sick, he is the one that has to cure you'. A person might be made sick by accident, if they stare at an *angangkere* maybe, or if they play with his hair or his hat without thinking.

The elder healers taught the clever ways to learn about healing, and taught about respect and taking care of families' wellbeing. And also respect for the wellbeing of the Land and everything in it – water, plants, animals, trees, people – everything including caves, hills and other sites. It has to be the healer with the knowledge of that country that gives you that power of healing. You could become a healer on your grandfather's country, (mother's father's country), or maybe on your other grandfather's country, or even your grandmothers' countries.

Angangkere when I was young

There were a few healers around when I was a young girl, people
who were there to heal the sick. There were a few women and men.
Like old Atnape-arenye, poor thing, he was a healer. When we were
sick he used to make us well. When I was a child I had bad sore ears
and I became deaf. We went to old Atnape-arenye and he helped
heal the sore ears. He started to feel around the ears with his hands,
then whatever it is that healers feel in their hands, the *arrwengkelthe*
(poison), whatever it was making my ears sore, he then threw away
towards a certain direction.

So old Atnape-arenye first rubbed his hands together, most
probably to get the power working. Then he put the palms of both
his hands against one of my ears, cupping it and pressing hard on the
ear, drawing out the *arrwengkelthe*. Then he slid his hands off my ear,
still cupping the *arrwengkelthe* in them, and blew onto the poison,
blowing it away, and then he wiped his hands of the poison, brushing
his hands against each other, like you would if your hands were dirty.
He did this with both my ears.

Then he sang the healing song over the ears. After singing my
ears with the healing song he told me to have a sleep. After sleeping,
I woke up and my ears were feeling a lot better. That's how they used
to heal things like sore ears. That is how our healers used to heal and
cure these types of ailments.

After using his hands to rub and heal with, and sometimes the
mouth to suck out the disease, the healer has to get rid of the diseases. So he or she points to the north, south, east, or westerly direction
then throws it towards whichever direction they prefer.

Old Atnape-arenye used to sing my ears with the healing song,
with the healing song for sore ears, whatever healing song from the
land that may have been. For example, the emu healing song and the

healing fat can be rubbed onto your ears, applying the healing fat and singing the healing song.

Old Atnape-arenye, he comes from Atnape, he lived there at Atnape. He and his wife were the people that knew about where the healing power comes from. They used to heal the family; they healed their families, not just anyone, maybe not a stranger that came and got sick. The healers only healed their own people, especially this old man. He was a great healer and very smart too. He was very special, you know, to heal some types of illnesses, and heal people quickly. These healers of ours, they know of the old illnesses we get. Those illnesses are the only ones that they cure. The sicknesses that they don't know about they leave well alone. The diseases people get nowadays are very different to the ones they are used to curing. The people in the early days used to catch smaller illnesses. Our healers used to cure them very quickly because they knew what made someone sick.

Old Atnape-arenye was given the healing power to heal the sick when he was a small child. His people that were the healers gave him the gift to heal others that become ill. Others also are recognized with the healing gift when they are still children. That's how it was, and it's still like that today.

There were a few other healers around when I was a young girl. There were a few women as well. One of the women healers was *mame-mame* (grandmother) Penangke, the poor thing, she was a great healer, very clever, and she also healed us when we got sick. When I was a child with those very bad ears, deaf as a doornail, the pus and muck running out of my ears, old *mame-mame* Penangke would help heal them as well.

The healers were clever. When someone was boned, or had an illness, or has been hurt in some way, or the northwest wind blew

– all these things make you ill – our healer was there to help make you well again. Snake bites as well, they used to heal them too, sometimes.

Awelye – Healing fat

The healing songs come from different places. They originate in the particular places that people know, and then spread out to other places with the same Dreaming. They are the healing powers – they belong to particular places. People don't use *awelye* belonging to other people's country – they only use *awelye* belonging to their own country. Whatever their own *awelye* Dreaming is – whether it is emu, perentie or kangaroo or whatever – that's the *awelye* that they use. They use the things that originated in their own country.

Healing fat songs are used to cure people when they become sick. The *awelye* – healing fat process – used different kinds of animal fat.

The special fats that were used for healing come from some animals that we eat. The elders in the early days used bush animal fats as a cure. Here are some names – emu, goanna, perentie. Nowadays people use bullock fat to make the *awelye* healing fat to rub onto the sick person to heal them. The fat that is made into dripping that you buy from the shops is being used now for healing by the younger healers.

The *awelye* healing is very important. The country, song, markings, the healing fat, and Dreamings are all involved, and connected to a person's four grandparents and their countries. From all these places we recognize the Dreamings from our relations – our mother's mothers, our mother's fathers, our father's fathers and our father's mothers. That is the reason we really know a lot about our traditional country and the healing powers that come from it. That's what it was like with our elders in those days, they had lots of knowledge about healing and cures.

The fat from emu, goanna or perentie is sung by the traditional healer, that's when it becomes the medicine. The *angangkere* sings the fat with the *awelye* totem songs from their country where they originated. Healing fat from the country where you have originated from, *apmere aknganentye-ngentyele*. Our healers were very special, clever people, and there's a few around today.

The healing power belongs to people who are chosen to become traditional healers. These people who are the traditional healers have their very own healing powers – they don't belong to anyone else. Like it might be a kangaroo healing power. Others have healing powers they get from animals like the wasp, emu, goanna, and porcupine. There's lots of other living things as well. The traditional healer sings the sick person after treating them with his or her hands first.

Ntyerlele uthneme – Boning

If a person is thought to have done the wrong thing by the *angangkere* – who is there to uphold the Law as well as to heal people – then the *angangkere* can punish them by boning them. If a person went to places that they're not allowed to be at, like a sacred site, they might get punished in this way. Or the *angangkere* might bone someone as a payback for something wrong the person did to the *angangkere* or his family. Only men use the bone as a punishment. The bone itself is made from the shin of the kangaroo, and they treat it with *arrwengkelthe* (magic poison) that can make the person sick. Sometimes the 'bone' can be made out of a small, slim mulga stick. They'll clean that up and then sing it with the *arrwengkelthe* and then use that to bone the person.

When a person gets boned, he or she first starts feeling that they've been boned. They might have a soreness or a pain coming on, and more-or-less straight away they'll think, 'Oh, somebody has boned me'. And then that person starts thinking to themselves, 'I'm sick because of the boning'. Then they lose their will to be strong and they really become very ill. Maybe they can will themselves to die. Because they really think that someone wants to kill them, and that person probably won't stop until they're dead. Like it's a payback.

The family of the sick person will always get *angangkere* to heal the one that's been boned, if it's not too late. The *angangkere* will either heal with the hands, or they'll find out with their hands where the sore is, and they'll suck out the bone or mulga stick that's entered into the sick person's body. Then they bury it in wet soil or throw it right away from the sick person, telling everybody around not to go near it, or it might infect them too with the *inngelhentye akngerre* (the contagious sickness).

After the bone has been taken out, the person starts feeling better. The traditional healer then sprinkles spit over the body after pulling the bone out, then rubs his hands with the healing powers over the sick person's body, and heals the wound from the bone by pressing on the skin so that is goes back to how it was. That is how our Ancestors did these healings. We still follow their footprints even today. The younger traditional healers now are still doing the same healing as their Ancestors did. The healing powers have been handed down from generation to generation to the rightful people.

Aretharre – Northwest wind

The northwest wind starts blowing at the beginning of Spring and that tells us that Summer is on its way. Sometimes the northwest wind, called *aretharre*, dries out the grasses and small plants, making it very dusty and causing the country to be a fire hazard.

The *aretharre* blows from the northwest. It makes you sick. 'That wind is a bad one', our elders used to say. When the northwest wind blows you must not walk around. If you go out in it instead of staying at home, you are asking to get sick. The wind has got something that makes you sick. If at that time you feel sick in the stomach or the head, that's because of the northwest wind going into you (*atwarentye akngerre*). When people get sick after walking in the northwest wind you must get a traditional healer to come and heal the person's stomach and head by touching them and singing them to make them well. The disease you get from the northwest wind is bad – it makes people very ill. So don't walk around in the northwest wind while it is blowing – wait until it stops blowing, then walk around. This wind is very hot and it's blowing up a lot of dust. This type of hot wind from the northwest makes you feel very tired and lazy (*arewampe*), making you not want to do anything. Some people get very irritable. *Awelye*, the healing song, is sung over the sick person, to make them well again.

The northwest wind is bad. It carries bad vibes, causing something like a rock to enter into your body, and making you ill. When you walk around in the northwest wind, you start to feel sharp pain in your stomach. That is when you go and see a healer who may be able to help you. As our elders used to say, 'Three little black rocks, they are the northwest wind's bad magic'.

Imatyawennge – Putting on curses

In Arrernte, when you use *imatyawennge* or *imamperle*, that's saying you put a curse on someone. 'Look at that *imamperle, imatyawennge*'. When you call someone '*imamperle*' that's means that you are putting a curse on that person and that may be a bad thing. Saying the words makes them come true, but only if you mean to put a curse on. You make it happen by saying those bad words, those names. A curse is not a good thing to use, and makes people sick. Anyone can put a curse on, they don't have to have special power like the *angangkere* does. The power is in the saying of the words.

Some of our healers used to cure illnesses that was caused by another's evil curse. If the healer you see doesn't cure you after the curse has been put on you, that healer may not be able to cure you at all. He or she may send you to the source that made your illness by that curse. The healer uses his or her hands, feeling, rubbing where it hurts or where it's sore, making it feel better. That is how it was done. The earlier healers were very good, their healing powers were strong.

Angangkere alhengke-aretyakenhe – Disrespecting *angangkere*

A really clever traditional healer can make a person sick or make a person well. Their special healing powers can make a sick person well or they can make a well person sick. It can even happen by accident. If you wear the hat belonging to a traditional healer your head will start aching. That means that the healer's powers have made you sick. If you go anywhere near a restricted sacred site then the traditional healer can put a spell on you and make you ill.

If someone keeps staring at the healer, as if you do not remember and do not recognize the healer, he or she can make you ill with their power. We are not recognizing the power the healer has got, if you don't recognize the healer and you keep looking at her or him. They curse you then, not really knowing they have done it, then you get ill. Our old people in the early days used tell us, 'Don't stare or look at a healer too much because the healer can make you sick with his or her power.' Even a small child who plays with a healer's hat – they can become sick. The healer's power is very strong. If the child put the hat on his or her head then they might be accidentally cursed and become sick. If you touch anything belonging to the healer, or even if the child puts the hat on someone else's head, that person can be cursed and become sick. Clothes or anything that's belonging to a healer cannot be played around with. You can't play with anything that is theirs or you are asking for trouble.

A person might become blind. If their eyes went blind, our elders used to say that the coal from the fire had entered into their eye. We say that something enters into your body and makes you sick, or gives you sores. When some sickness or whatever enters into your body and makes you sick – we call that *atwareme*. That's what we call *atwareme* – the process of making someone sick by using traditional powers.

Treatments and Conditions

Some 'flus are bad – you have to get a traditional healer with his healing power to sing and heal with his hands. Other people might be too sick to heal quickly, and it takes the healer a lot longer to make them well. But other 'flus and sicknesses can be cured by just using bush medicines, without needing to see the healer. In the early station days there weren't other medicines around, like European's medicines, for some of these sicknesses. But there were plenty of bush medicines around, just like the old days when our Ancestors lived. We still do the same thing with the bush medicines like they did. These medicines are only good for some illnesses though. Aboriginal people make up these medicines and use them. Some of our younger people are using these medicines still. Our traditional healers taught us that the medicine plants get their power from the Land, just like they themselves do.

Utyene alhewentye akngerre –
Washing Medicines

Arrethe
rock fuchsia bush, *Eremophila freelingii*

Arrethe is a medicine that was used by our elders – it's good to cure a few different conditions. It is better to collect these medicines after rain because they are more potent then. The leaves are shining with the gum seeping through and they are very sticky. When people pick the branches, the leaves let out a very strong aroma because, around this time of the season, the medicine is strongest, after a slight bit of rain.

The native fuchsia medicine leaves are collected then ground, put in water for the sick to drink and wash in, making the sick person well again. *Arrethe* is good for bad 'flu. When it's rubbed on like Vicks, it can even heal someone that has chest 'flu that's very rattly, and is finding it hard to breathe. If a person's body is aching with the 'flu, you collect the *arrethe* leaves, grind the raw leaves, then

LEFT: A selection of grinding stones. Arrernte people used to leave the bigger stone at camping areas such as *Anthwerrke* and *Akapulye*, buried in the ground or turned upside down to protect the grinding surface from the weather. The smaller stone would be carried when people travelled from place to place.
Photo courtesy Ada Nano.

RIGHT: Preparing to grind, with a coolamon for collecting the plants, a billy of water and grinding stones.
Photo courtesy Ada Nano.

apply the green liquid onto where it's aching. You can also put the leaves in water and boil it for the sick person to bathe in and make his or her body healthy and strong again. The leaves of the *arrethe* are also burned, making smoke so that the sick person can sit near it and inhale the smoke to make him or her well. That is how our Ancestors did it in the past, and there's people who are still using these same medicine today.

Arrethe

Atnyerlenge
crimson turkey bush, *Eremophila latrobei*

Atnyerlenge leaves are collected then ground, then the green juice from the leaves is applied onto the body. The flowers of this bush have honey in the Spring. Aboriginal people suck the honey out of these flowers, which is a good medicine for sore throats. The juice of the leaves is also good when rubbed onto the body, or rubbed on the head for headaches, making the person well.

Aherre-intenhe
harlequin fuchsia, red poverty bush, *Eremophila duttonii*

Aherre-intenhe leaves are collected, put in water and boiled, then used to wash sick people with. That's how these medicines were used in the early days to heal the sick. *Aherre-intenhe* leaves can also be ground, and the green juice from the leaves is then applied onto the body, maybe on your aching legs or arms. This medicine is good for that.

When a child has got sores on his or her head, you wash him or her with the *aherre-intenhe* and apply the leaf juice like an ointment onto the sore, so it will mend back to its original state. That's how the people lived in those times, washing and applying these medicines onto their bodies.

These three plants, *arrethe*, *atnyerlenge* and *aherre-intenhe* are mostly all mixed together and are used as an antiseptic wash. The leaves are collected then ground and placed in water to make the medicine. These three *Eremophilas* are often used in this way, all together. *Arrethe* and *atnyerlenge* grow everywhere on stony hills. *Aherre-intenhe* grows on the road to Amoonguna on the gravelly flat. There they grow really bushy. The leaves of the *Eremophila* are collected, mixed all together, and then ground and used. That's how we use these plants to make our medicines.

Aherre-intenhe

Utnerrenge

The leaves are stripped from the *utnerrenge* in preparation for grinding.

Water is added and mixed with the ground *utnerrenge* leaves.

The resulting liquid is used as a treatment for burns and sores.

Utnerrenge
emu bush, *Eremophila longifolia*

Utnerrenge medicine is good for sores. You gather a few leaves and grind them, then the green liquid from the leaves is applied onto sores or burns to stop them from weeping. It dries out the burn or sore. It's also very good for scabies.

Athenge, atyarnpe
ironwood, *Acacia estrophiolata*

The ironwood tree's root bark was used as a medicine by our elders as an eye wash for sore eyes. It's good for other sores as well. You dig the roots then pound them with a rock, and peel the bark off and place it in water and boil it up. The water will turn red from the bark. The water that's turned red is the medicine for sores.

Digging for the roots of *athenge*.

Arlketyerre
dead finish, *Acacia tetragonophylla*

The dead finish tree roots are also used for medicine. Aboriginal people dig for the roots under the foot of the tree. Then the roots are pounded with a rock to loosen up the bark so that it will peel off easily. This is then soaked in water, and can be boiled to make an antiseptic wash, or an antiseptic-type solution to apply to skin irritations, boils, sores, abrasions, and also for sore eyes. That is how our elders taught and showed us how these medicines were made and used. Now we teach our young ones about these medicines. The dead finish tree root makes the water red when you soak it or boil it. This red water is the medicine to wash any type of sore with.

Apere arntape
river red gum bark, *Eucalyptus camaldulensis var. obtusa*

Apere bark is collected, then it's pounded into a mash and put in water to make an antiseptic for a mouth wash or sore eyes. It is also good for wounds. The bark is full of the gum, and it is that gum that is the medicine that is used to cure sore eyes and for wounds and other types of sores.

The inner soft bark of the red river gum is very sticky. The gum, called *apere alhwe* (gumtree blood) is collected when the soft inner bark is pounded with a rock. The mash you make from it is then mixed with water to use as an antiseptic, and to wash sores with. Aboriginal people didn't have tins or billycans to use to boil things in, even to boil medicines. Tin cans and billycans were bought in by the early settlers when they came to this country. Aboriginal people made and used these medicines for a long time. When they didn't have tin cans they used small scoops to make the medicines in, to apply onto whatever type of sore people had.

You can wash in the water from the bark of the river gum. It's good for soaking in too, that helps the skin heal, and become well. That's how our people made this medicine.

Arlketyerre

Apere

Grinding the bark of *arlketyerre* roots.

Arlkerrke – meat ants

Meat ants are another source of antiseptic that was used for sore eyes, like
when children get mucky eyes. The
meat ant solution is good to pour into
the eye like an eye drop that heals the
eye as well.

You collect the black ants by dis-
turbing their nest. When the ants all
come up out of their holes, you trample
them with your feet. After that you
collect the dead ants and place them
into water for a short time. Then the
ants are pulled out of the water and
the solution is then used to wash sore
eyes with, and the sore eye clears up
very quickly. Ant solution was even
used to wash clean someone who is
blind, or someone that gets bung eyes
from flies. Mother's breast milk was
also used to cure some eyes. There's
lots of these meat ants everywhere here
on the Land. This is a medicine that
Aboriginal people used for centuries,
and it's still being used today.

Arlkerrke

OPPOSITE: Veronica Dobson standing by a big
old *apere* (red river gum) at *Anthwerrke* (Emily
Gap). The older the tree, the better the sap.

Arrkernke gum (arrkapere)
bloodwood, *Corymbia opaca*

Some gums from trees are a medicine, others are a chewing gum that's eaten, and others are used as glue for things. I remember the medicine from the bloodwood tree – it's like the ironwood tree gum. The ironwood gum is eaten, but you can't eat the bloodwood gum, because it's a medicine. The gum from the bloodwood seeps out from the trunk of the tree, and when it is still fresh and runny, it is collected and applied onto sores. If the gum has dried out, it is gathered and mixed with water to wash people that might have skin irritations – that gum is a real good medicine. The old dry gum looks like jelly crystals and when it is collected from under the tree it is ground up and mixed with water to make a paste, or just used in a powder form, to put on burns.

The gum is good for other types of sores as well and even for sore eyes. You put the gum into water and use it as a wash. The water can also be used as a mouth wash and as a gargle for sore throats. People gargle and rinse their throat and mouth by pouring the liquid into their mouth, and making a bubbling noise in the back of their throat. It's good medicine, the bloodwood gum.

OPPOSITE: Veronica Dobson with a *arrkernke* (bloodwood tree) at *Anthwerrke* (Emily Gap). Photo courtesy author and CLC.

Arrwatnurlke
striped mint bush, *Prostanthera striatiflora*

Arrwatnurlke is a medicine that people in the early days used a lot.
People collected the striped mint bush leaves and mashed them
up with a rock, making them into medicine for sores. You splash
drops of water onto the leaves while you're grinding, to make more
of the leaf juice, and then drip the juice onto the sores. This is a
medicine also used for people who have bad 'flus or aching body,
and it helps the sick to get well quickly. The *arrwatnurlke* medicine
is very important – it helped many people get well, when there were
no other medicines around in those old days. There's lots of these
striped mint bushes growing all over these central areas. In Spring
the leaves of the mint bush shine with the resin seeping through
the leaves. Aboriginal people collect the sticky leaves from the mint
bush then grind them into a mash. The green liquid is then rubbed
onto the body – that's how they used these medicines. This plant
medicine is also good for venereal diseases and scabies. The medicine
is used as a wash or as an ointment for these types of illness.

Arrwatnurlke grows on the side of ranges, creeks, gullies, and on
small hills. These medicines are from here, they are part of us, and
they are still very important to our people.

The leaves of the *arrwatnurlke* are ground and mixed with water.

To the left of the grinding stone, the small yellow fruits of the *utyerrke* (bush fig) are sitting on the ball of paste made from the powdered *utyerrke*.

Arrwatnurlke

Aherre–aherre

Irlweke
white cypress pine, *Callitris glaucophylla*
Some people collect the leaves of the white
cypress pine, crush them by grinding, and place
them in water to boil. The hot water is then
used to apply on, or wash with, if your body is
itchy, and it's used to rub onto the chest when
you get bad chest 'flu.

Aherre-aherre
native lemon grass, *Cymbopogon ambiguus*
Always people used the lemon grass to make
their medicine. The people in the early days
never had tins, but had small scoops. The *aherre-
aherre* was ground, then placed in a small scoop
of water and drunk. The lemon grass dries out
and dies, but it grows back very quickly when it
rains. The elders used to collect the green lemon
grass from around the base of the dead clump,
and pounded it to use to rub onto the body
to make it well.

Irlweke

   For people who may get the 'flu bad, their chest is very rattly,
some colds are like that. The lemon grass is then placed in water and
boiled, then you give a small amount to the person with the 'flu to
drink. After drinking the medicine the person sleeps, making him or
her feel well. Other 'flus are very bad, and the healer is the only one
that can help heal the sick by singing the healing song. In the hills,
aherre-aherre grow everywhere, especially in gullies.

Apernentye akngerre – Ointments

The early days people (*arrwekelenye mape*) used to use goanna fat, perentie fat, emu fat and porcupine fat. They used to mix these fats with the traditional medicines. These fats are very important for rubbing on sick people to make them well.

Aherre-intenhe
harlequin fuchsia, red poverty bush, *Eremophila duttonii*
The *aherre-intenhe* leaves were ground, mixed with fat, and used as an ointment or sticky paste to rub onto people's chests, when they suffer from bad 'flus. Also for aches and pains, or muscle soreness.

Pintye-pintye
apple bush, *Pterocaulon serrulatum*
Pintye-pintye is a favoured medicine for people with very bad 'flu. This medicine is made into a Vicks-like ointment. You collect the leaves, grind it and add fat to it, then rub it onto the body, chest, back, and on aching bones. This medicine is also used for head 'flu.

Arrwatnurlke
striped mint bush, *Prostanthera striatiflora*
Here is another medicine that people used to mixed with fat. You collect the leaves then grind them, then mix them with fat and rub the mixture onto the body. When people get bad 'flu and their body is aching, you rub this medicine onto them.

Pintye-pintye

Untyeye

Mixing the burnt bark of *untyeye* with water after it has been ground.

Untyeye
fork-leafed corkwood, *Hakea divaricata*

You go looking for the corkwood tree. You see them growing on sides of hills or river banks, and on flat country. You find the corkwood, then peel the bark and burn it.

The charcoal is then taken out of the fire and covered with soft soil to cool it down. Then the burnt corkwood is crushed, and ground into a powder. Then it's applied onto a little child's heat rash. Young babies get heat rashes in the Summer when they sweat. Heat rashes break out when baby sweats around his or her neck. If the baby is fat, he or she sweats under the armpit, around the groin, then heat rash develops around the neck, and the groin gets red raw. That why you use the black powder from the bark of the corkwood. It dries out the heat rash and helps it to heal up quicker. You can apply the corkwood bark just as a powder form, or mix it with fat and then apply it.

This medicine is black, and that's how people made and have always used this medicine to cure sores and other skin irritations. This type of medicine was made to heal all types of sores by applying directly onto them. The sore might be getting bigger and bigger. The corkwood is used to put onto sores that are spreading and clear them up. The corkwood bark medicine is also good for babies with sore mouths from sucking, and for women with sore nipples. The corkwood bark powder is applied on to the sore nipples so that the breast will heal. That's how our elders used do these things, and now we are still carrying out the same thing, making those medicines like they did.

Kwertele-ilentye akngerre – Smoking and Inhalations

Utnerrenge
emu bush, *Eremophila longifolia*

The emu bush medicine is used for smoking. You dig a hole, make a small fire in the hole, then gather the leaves of the emu bush and place the leaves on the fire to make the smoke. The sick person is placed over the smouldering hole.

The emu bush medicine was also used for smoking an *irlkngaye* (newborn baby) to make him or her strong. You get the newborn baby and lay him or her into the smoke of the smouldering leaves of the emu bush, so that the child will grow up strong and healthy. The mother has to smoke herself as well, to help her make milk for her newborn baby, and to heal herself after giving birth. That's how the smoking was done.

In the early days when a child got measles and got very sick, the elders smoked the child with the leaves of the emu bush. After the child has been smoked, he or she sleeps, making themselves better. When they wake up, they feel a lot better after the smoking treatment. Some adults were smoked to make them sweat when they got bad 'flus. That's how our elders used to treat their illnesses and cure their people. People are still using these medicines today for various ailments.

Arrwatnurlke
striped mint bush, *Prostanthera striatiflora*

The *arrwatnurlke* leaves are collected then burnt to make smoke. The sick person sits on the side of where the smoke is drifting, to inhale the smoke. After inhaling, the person sleeps, and when he or she wakes up they feel a lot better. That is how our elders showed and taught us about these medicines, how they were used when we were still pretty young. We show the younger people now how to make and use these medicines, so that they will know about them and continue to use them, and teach others how to make and use them.

If we are sick, we make ourselves better by sitting upwind from a fire and inhaling the medicinal smoke from *arrwatnurlke*. This can cure headaches. Newborn babies are smoked to make their bodies strong.

Sometimes traditional medicines are collected by Aboriginal people and made into a pillow to sleep on, so that they can inhale the aroma of the medicinal plant, and make themselves better while they are sleeping.

Aherre-intenhe
harlequin fuchsia bush, red poverty, *Eremophila duttonii*

Aherre-intenhe leaves are used for medicine purposes, for 'flus and other ailments. A person who's sick with bad body 'flu, his or her body aches and pains. You collect the leaves from this fuchsia and burn them making them smoulder and smoke, making sure that the sick person sits near the smoke to inhale the fumes and sweat it out, make him or her feel better. This also works for a child or an adult that may have bad chest 'flu and can't breath properly. For sick people, others make pillows out of the leaves of the *aherre-intenhe*, so that the sick one can lay on it and inhale the fumes, then feel a lot better when he or she wakes up. Then they can breathe more easily.

Arrethe
rock fuchsia bush, *Eremophila freelingii*

The *arrethe* leaves are burnt, and the smoke is inhaled by the sick person. Then, after inhaling the smoke, he or she sleeps it off. When the person wakes up, he or she feels a lot better. This is not how the elders in the early days used to make this medicine, this is a new way to use *arrethe*. The old people used to use *arrethe* as a wash and a rub.

Veronica Dobson with a coolamon and a clump of *aherre-aherre* (lemon grass).

Pintye-pintye
apple bush, *Pterocaulon serrulatum*
The *pintye-pintye* leaves can be collected and made into a pillow, so that the sick person with a blocked nose or a chest infection can sleep on it, inhaling the fumes. When he or she wakes up they will feel a lot better. Also, the apple bush medicine leaves are collected when they have dried out, and then they're burned for the sick person to inhale, for a person who might have head 'flu, so he or she can inhale the smoke.

Arrernte people used to collect the *pintye-pintye* and roll the leaves into balls and shove them into nooks and crannies around the inside of their *ilthes* (humpies). This was to keep the air inside sweet and fresh, and also it was believed that they would keep away 'flus and other sickness.

Aherre-aherre
native lemon grass, *Cymbopogon ambiguus*
Aherre-aherre is good for 'flus mainly. This lemon grass is good for people to inhale when they get aches and pains, or when people catch the 'flu. You collect the lemon grass then make it into a pillow, the sick person can sleep on it and inhale the fumes of the lemon grass, so as to make themselves feel well.

The lemon grass is used when it's dry too, that's good. You crush it in your hand then sniff it if you have head 'flus, and it helps fix your head. *Aherre-aherre* is used when it's green as well. You collect the lemon grass medicine and crush it in your hand and it lets out a strong smell. This medicine is good for 'flus.

Utyene arlenye-ilentye akngerre – Drying Agents

The plants used for this, *arrwatnurlke* (mint bush), and *utnerrenge* (emu bush), are used in a similar way. The leaves are ground, and the juices are used to sprinkle onto sores. The leaf juice burns when it's applied onto open wounds, and that's what dries out the sore, helping it to heal. Just like the hospital medicines iodine or mercurochrome. Corkwood bark is also used for drying out sores. The bark is first burned, and then ground, and the black powder is used to apply onto weeping sores to dry them out.

Arltunga

Ltyentye

Drawing ointments

Ltyentye
beefwood tree,
Grevillea striata
From the beefwood tree you
collect the gum, it seeps out
of the limbs of these trees
just like it does out of the
bloodwood. This gum is what
the medicine is made from.
For boils you collect the gum,
grind it, and mix it with water
into a paste. The paste is used
as a drawing agent, making the
boil burst and heal.

Arrkernke **gum (***arrkapere***)**
– bloodwood,
Corymbia opaca
The old dry gum that looks
like jelly crystals is collected
from under the tree. It is
ground up and mixed with
water to make a paste. The
paste is also applied onto boils,
making them like a scab, to
draw the pus out that's making
it ache and sore.

Sap from *Ityentye* ready to be collected
for grinding.

Traditional Bandages

Irrkenthe –
Bag shelter of itchy grub,
Ochrogaster contraria
The bag shelter of the itchy grub is found on lots of different trees. The *irrkenthe* is collected from the tree, and cleaned out properly to get rid of the droppings, skin and hair that might be left in the bag. After the bag has been cleaned, you then peel it into strips. Then you get the soft silk inner bag to use like a bandage for burns. You cover the sore for a few days with the itchy grub bag, and apply emu bush leaf liquid onto the sore as well. The sore from the fire heals up quicker when you apply the emu bush medicine. That's how

An *irrkenthe*, the shelter constructed by the itchy grub, found in certain species of trees.
Photo courtesy Ada Nano.

it was done by our elders. In a few days you'll see that sore getting better. Sores after a fire-burn were taken care of by the elders. The itchy grub bag is an important thing for burns. Contact with eyes, nose, mouth or skin causes irritations and swelling and must be avoided when cleaning the itchy grub's bag. It can make you break out in lumps all over. Be careful and wash your hands after handling the itchy grub's bag. That's how our elders did these things before Europeans in the early days.

Ahelhe urinpe – Hot soil

After a tiny baby is born, the elders cut the ayepe (umbilical cord) off. Our elders cut the umbilical cord, then tied it in a knot very soon after the baby is born. The navel is called *tyelepelepe*. After cutting the cord and tying it, you get the hot sand from the fireplace, put it into a cloth bag, then place it onto the baby's stomach. It works like a hot water bottle, and it dries out the belly button and also heals it well. That is how our elders used the hot soil from the fire – like a hot water bottle. Arrernte women are still giving birth to their babies at home, and they are still using the same process to heal the baby's navel after getting rid of the umbilical cord. Our people are still using these same healing methods today, like our Ancestors did.

You must tie the cut-off part of the *ayepe* around the child's neck like a necklace – that's how it was done by our elders. Otherwise, they believe, the child would miss his or her cord and fret and get sick. That's how it was always done according to Aboriginal Law. That's what's done with the cord of a new baby. So that the child grows up with the umbilical cord still tied to his or her neck, until the cord dries and breaks and falls off.

Hot soil is also used as a hot water bottle for aching boils or ears. The hot soil from the fire is collected and put into a bag or a cloth. It is used to place onto a boil that's been aching all night. It works to ease off the aching and the soreness. That's how it was done in the early days by the elders. If your ears were sore and aching, the same process is done. The hot soil is also used for some people who often suffer with aches and pains like arthritis.

Antyeye itnyetyeke mpwareme – Sweating treatments

Irlweke
white cypress pine, *Callitris glaucophylla*

The white cypress pine was used by our elders in the early days.
They collected the bark then laid it out as a bed, then they used to
lay the sick person onto the sticky fresh bark. The rest of the bark is
then wrapped over the top of the person like a blanket, so they can
get well after lying between the barks and sweat it out. This is used
when you have a very bad touch of the 'flu, when your body aches
and pains, or you get a fever with hot and cold flushes and you're
unable to do anything. That is how the elders treated their sick then.
The white cypress pine is also used to tie around people's stomachs if
they have stomach problems and that heals it. The inner bark of the
white cypress pine is peeled off, and then that's used.

Ikwentyele aletye mwerre-ileme –
Healing deep wounds with ashes

Ritual violence is done in mourning. This includes the punishment of certain relatives of the deceased. People cut themselves – *aletye* (sorry cuts) – when they are sorry after a death in their family. The family of the deceased person goes through the ritual punishment and sheds blood for their dead. That is how it was always done and is still being done today. The Law has been that way all the time. Some people are still practising this ritual punishment when one of their relatives or a child dies. Some sorry cuts might be fairly deep, when the person cuts themselves to shed blood for the loss of a family member. *Ikwentye, arlpmenye* (ashes) are then put onto the wound to stop the bleeding. You get the white ash from the fireplace, pour it into the wound and press it down with your hand into the deep wound. The wound would heal and mend back to it's original state, leaving a scar. That's how these wounds were treated by the elders. Other deep wounds are treated by applying ashes to them in the same way as *aletye*. People still have strong Law and the mourning rituals are still practised today.

Itelye mwerre-ilentye akngerre – Curing warts

Arlketyerre
dead finish, *Acacia tetragonophylla*

The dead finish tree leaves are a medicine that is used for warts. The needle-like leaves of the dead finish are picked, and then used to poke into the wart, making the wart bleed. The leaves are pulled out, and then the wart dries out and disappears within a few days. Some people say you get warts from frogs. Frogs don't give you warts, you just seem to get lots of these wart-like things appearing on your skin, like freckles on people's faces, legs, arms and other parts of their body. The warts are treated with the leaves of the dead finish and cleared up, mainly on the soft parts of your skin, not on the palms of the hands or soles of the feet. That is how our elders used this cure to clear the wart.

Veronica Dobson beside an *arlketyerre*.

The spiny leaves of
arlketyerre are inserted
under a wart.
Photo courtesy Ada Nano.

Arlketyerre

Ngkwerne ultakelhentye – Broken bones

The traditional healer is usually the one who deals with broken bones. First he has to calm and lay the person down. When people break their arm or leg, you must lay them down then, keep them quiet or still, so that the bones don't break any more. The person will have to lay very still. Then the healer sings the healing song over the broken bone. The song of the perentie is the song that's used to heal the broken bone. After that, splints are made. Two straight sticks from the *arne ilwempe* (ghost gum) are collected and placed one on each side of the broken bone. These are then tied on to the arm or leg with inner bark from mainly the *arne atnyeme* (witchetty bush) or *arne artetye* (mulga). The roots of these trees were dug up and cut. Then the outer bark was stripped off the root, and the inner bark fibres ripped out and used as a string. When these fibres are wet with sap, they are easy to use as string.

LEFT: Collecting the inner bark fibres from the roots of *arne atnyeme*.

OPPOSITE TOP: The bark fibres of *arne atnyeme* tie on a finger splint.

OPPOSITE BOTTOM: A leg splint in place, using bark fibres of *arne atnyeme* to tie on sticks from the *arne ilwempe*.

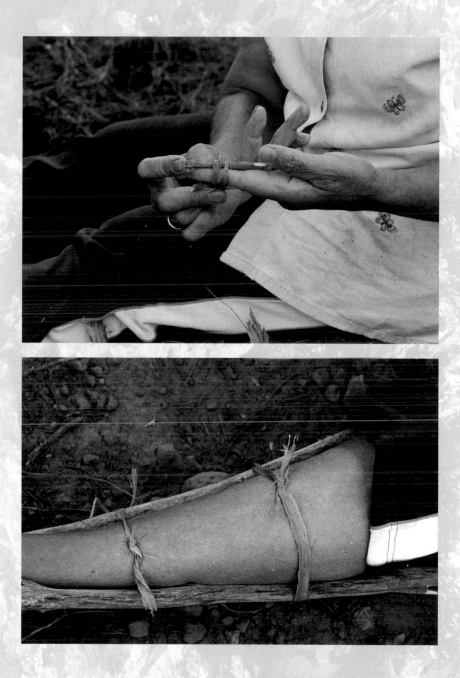

The sap of arne ilwempe is eaten but it is not a medicine.
Its branches are used for splints.

The splints were bound around the broken bone, maybe in three
places along the limb. The wet bark string will shrink as it dries out,
and hold the splint tightly in place so the person can use their arm
or leg in a little while. It's important that you don't tie the splints
too tight to begin with, so that the blood can run freely through the
broken limb, instead of swelling up. You should also make sure that
you keep an eye on the person to see if he or she is all right.

Sometime *irrketye* (hairstring) is used to tie the splints on. This
is made from human hair or animal fur, and is rolled on the thigh to
make into lengths.

Apmwe-iperre – Snakebite

Snakebites were treated by *angangkere*, or by anyone who might have been around when you were bitten by a snake. You had to work quickly to tie a *irrketye* (hairstring) around the limb above from where you was bitten to stop the poison blood from flowing through your body. People always wore their hairstrings either as an *atyepe* (belt) or as a headband. If you needed to tighten the hairstring, you put a stick through the string and twitched it up tight.

Then down where the limb was bitten, a cut was made with a knife or any other sharp instrument that was on hand, and the bad blood was made to flow out, by squeezing the leg or arm. Sometimes people used to suck the blood out of the wound, as long as they didn't have a tooth problem or any soreness in the mouth. They would have poisoned themselves otherwise. After bleeding, the wound was cleaned with water or wiped with the soft inner bark from some tree roots. The person was made to lie down then, and people kept an eye on them to make sure that he or she didn't begin to lose consciousness or convulse. Sometimes, if they had a traditional healer, an *angangkere*, around, the traditional healer would sing the healing song over the wound, and would keep an eye over the person to make sure that the poison hadn't travelled any further than when the string was tied. If people acted quickly enough, usually the person would survive.

I have known about a few Arrernte people who have been bitten by snakes, but I've never known anyone to die from it. People were generally bitten on the hand or the lower leg, and others always worked very quickly to deal with snakebite. Our people always respected snakes by leaving them well alone.

This is how it was done before European medicine. Nowadays, medicine probably has a better way of treating snakebites. So you should follow the modern medicine way, not the old Arrernte way for this.

Losing weight

Atnetye
roots of the bush banana, silky pear, *Marsdenia australis*
The elders used to tell us that the bush banana plant roots are supposed to make you thin. If you eat too much of the roots it makes you too skinny. When we were kids we always used to dig the bush banana roots to eat. The bush banana roots are not like the yam – there's a long hard stick in the middle of the watery flesh, which you throw away. You don't eat that part – just the soft watery flesh on the outer part. You eat the banana roots raw or you can cook and eat them. They have a sweet and unusual taste, like licorice.

Peeled roots of *atnetye*.

Atnetye

Atne-irrkepe-akerte – Curing constipation

Awele-awele, alperrantyeye
bush tomato, *Solanum ellipticum*

The bush tomato plant has two names in different Arrernte dialects – *awele-awele*, and *alperrantyeye*. When it's Spring, the bush tomatoes are collected and eaten by people off the bushes. If you eat too many this way you end up with *atnelthe* (diarrhoea). The bush tomato works like a laxative and opens up your bowel. When people eat these bush tomatoes it cleans their stomach out, making them go to the toilet more. When the bush tomatoes ripen up they get yellowish in colour and you can smell the aroma from the ripe fruit in the distance.

If you eat a lot of bush tomato it makes your lips, mouth, tongue and teeth brown from the acid in the fruit. The bush tomatoes are collected when they ripen on the bush. The bush tomato can also be cooked in hot sand in the fire, and then eaten just as a food, not a medicine. That way you don't get *atnelthe* from it. Our elders cooked the sun-ripened fruit in the fire and ate them in this way – that is how people in the early days processed their foods. The younger people of today don't do this any more, cooking the bush tomatoes in the fire before eating them, not like the elders used to. If you feel sick in the stomach and constipated, you eat bush tomato raw and it will make your stomach loosen up, and make you go to the toilet. Don't give little children too many of the bush tomatoes to eat because it will give them diarrhoea, and could make them very sick.

OPPOSITE: Country around *Ltyentye Apurte* (Santa Teresa).

Atnelthe-irreme – Curing diarrhoea

Utyerrke
bush fig, *Ficus platypoda*

The seeds of the bush fig are a medicine for *atnelthe*. When a small child gets bad diarrhoea our elders collect the dried seeds from bush figs that have fallen to the ground, and grind them into a powder form. That's what was given to the child. While mother is breast-feeding her baby, the *utyerrke* powder is poured into the child's mouth, little by little, while he or she is feeding on the breast. So that the child can drink both the milk and the powder of the *utyerrke* together. That's how they did it in the early days when there weren't any European medicines around. The elders mixed the *utyerrke* powder into a paste with water for children with diarrhoea to eat, to help them get better, and also to make their stomach strong and stop them from getting sick.

Grinding the fruit of *utyerrke*.

After it is ground it is mixed with water.

Utyerrke

Toothache

Awele-awele, alperrantyeye
bush tomato, *Solanum ellipticum*
The bush tomato plant roots are used to cure toothaches. When the tooth aches all night it makes your face swell. Teeth can ache and make you very irritable too if it aches all night, not letting you sleep. Because of that, you get the fresh stem from the bush tomato. You dig the roots of the bush tomato, then you bake the root in the ash for a minute or two to warm up, then peel the skin and place it onto where the tooth is aching. After the aching has stopped, take the root out of your mouth.

Atnyerlenge
crimson turkey bush, *Eremophila latrobei*
The fresh green tip from the stems of the *atnyerlenge* is collected, peeled and poked into the sore tooth to stop the soreness and the aching of the tooth. The stem tip is left in the teeth for a short time or until the ache goes away, then it's pulled out. That's how it was done in the early days.

Ahelhe urinpe
hot soil
Hot soil was also used for an aching tooth. It was placed in a cloth and laid on the side of your face where it's aching.

Akarnteme – Headache

When people got headache, they tied either a vine called *arretherrke* (snake vine, *Tinospora smilacina*) or a *irrketye* (hairstring), around their forehead. They tied these reasonably tight around their head to stop it from aching. Sometimes, they slept while wearing the *arratherrke* or *irrketye*, and when they woke up they felt better. Most headaches were treated that way. Both the *arratherrke* and the *irrketye* are supposed to have some medicine potency in them to help the headache go away. The reason why the *irrketye* is believed to have potency is because it usually came from a powerful healer. Headache was never all that big a problem before our people started drinking alcohol.

Rlkerte lyetenye – sickness nowadays

Now there's lots of other, new illnesses that make people from this country sick. The food that is eaten is fatty. Also drinking too much grog makes them sick. Nowadays there are lots of sweet things that our elders never ate or drank. Our elders in the early days never got these sicknesses – blood pressure, or no kidney problems, no lung or liver problems, or overweight problems. They didn't know about these, didn't know about these sicknesses. People only got sick when they got too old – that's how they lived. The younger generation is always sick with these types of sicknesses. Lots of our people have died through having kidney, lung, liver, and blood problems, and from eating fatty foods and also from drinking too much alcohol. Our traditional healers can't cure people who are alcoholics – only whiteman's medicines will help cure these sicknesses.

Some of these other diseases that people get nowadays are very bad – cancer, disease of the heart, blood problems, kidney problems. These are the types of diseases that our people are suffering with now. It's because of the lifestyle they live now, easy access to booze, fatty foods and meats from bullocks, lambs, pigs and chickens. These are the types of things that are causing them to be ill. Men, women, some of them get swollen hearts and stomachs from drinking too much. Others get too fat because they eat the wrong food all the time. People must look after themselves. There's lots of diseases that people get nowadays that are life-threatening.

Looking south from *Akeyulerre* (Billy Goat Hill) to *Ntaripe* (Heavitree Gap).
Opposite: Today – *Akeyulerre* is on the edge of Alice Springs central business district. *Photo Margaret McDonell.*
Below: The olden days – a view of open country, taken from the same vantage point, between 1916 and 1924. *Photo courtesy Powell-Price Collection.*

Diabetes

Lots of Aboriginal people suffer with diabetes, you even see little children with it. The disease gets into their blood stream, because the children are fed with cool drinks and other foods that are no good for them. You see a woman pouring cool drink into a baby's bottle and giving it to the baby and the little one gets addicted to it. The child gets so used to eating and drinking sweet things. Instead of giving the child water or milk to drink, the mother gives it sweets all the time. Just because he or she is mother's favourite, always getting sweets. Which is making him or her sick, the child crying for sweet things and the mother keeps giving it to the child, instead of giving the child good food like apples or oranges, bananas or even green vegetables to eat. No, the mother keeps giving the child sweets. That's no good for the child.

The child is still very young when they start tasting sweets like cool drink, lollies, and other no-good foods. That's why the young children of today are always sick, because they haven't been taught to eat green vegetable like bush banana, bush orange, yams, and other foods like witchetty, kangaroo, perentie, goanna. That's just some of the bush foods – there's lots more. There's a lot that young people don't know about, the younger parents of today. They feed their children sweets and spoil them. The children get too used to sweets, and expect them all the time.

These types of diseases like diabetes are only getting recognized now by Aboriginal people – only when they see their relatives go down with the disease. Other Aboriginal people get a shock when they find out that they have already got the disease themselves. When you don't know about the disease and you feel you are getting sick, tell someone straight away, before it gets too bad.

There's lots of bad diseases nowadays that people get, like heart problems, kidney problems, liver problems. Aboriginal people get cancer too now. That's how it is nowadays. Our elders in the early days didn't know about these diseases. The younger generations are the ones getting these types of sicknesses, and the European healers are the ones that take care of them, helping them get better. Our Ancestors had their own healers that cured them and made them well, taking care of the sick.

I thought about the dialysis. What do Aboriginal people think about dialysis? What do you think, is this type of thing good or bad? Europeans take care of these kidney patients, keeping them going, the ones that make themselves sick through drinking. They keep them alive, looking after them, the ones that are on the dialysis, you know. Aboriginal people in the early days let their people die with some types of illnesses, and nowadays they got machines to look after them, keeping them alive.

Ampwerrke akngerre – Overweight

Some of the nowadays diseases are very bad, for overweight people, old people and young children, so you must look after yourselves. Because of some illnesses that are here now, you have to think of your bodies. Keep an eye on your child – if they're overweight and getting fatter their heart gets no good and the child suffers with breathing problems. His or her heart can be covered with thick fat that causes problems too – maybe finding it hard to breath – and that type of thing is no good for the child. Teach your child to eat good foods, and teach them how to eat fatty foods in moderation, not to eat them every day. Foods like chicken, chips, battered fish.

People buy lots of things that are sold, that are bad for them to eat all the time. Aboriginal people get sick because they eat too many fatty foods and drink too many sweet drinks, including grog.

People eat too much, not being active and just sitting around. Maybe clean up the camp, not just sitting around not being active, jumping in a car not wanting to walk, that is how they become lazy. That is why they are not healthy. Our elders always walked around wherever they had to go, and they were slim, trim and healthy people, strong and solid, that is how they were. People of today are big, fat and unhealthy, with the food they eat making themselves sick, also drinking booze.

Because of the white influence, the younger generation have to live with lots of shops where it's easy food, just pay and eat. They don't look out for themselves. Don't always buy lots of rubbish food and eat it all at once. Go walkabout too after eating and keep healthy. Go walking to make yourself healthy. Don't sit around at home all the time. Look after your body and keep healthy. If you have sores, keep your body clean, and if you feel sick, go to the clinic, see a health worker, about how you feel in your body. Your body is very overweight, how can I lose weight and be thinner? Go on a diet – that is the only way to lose weight.

Don't eat until you feel sick, don't be greedy, gutsing yourself with lots of food. That could be why some of these people have weight problems. Booze is another. People that drink booze, their stomach swells, looking like if they are pregnant. If you drink booze all the time your stomach swells and the kidneys, liver, lungs, heart as well, all collapses from booze poisoning. Our elders in the early days were proud, strong people, not like our people of today.

Ngkwarle – Alcohol

Nowadays, what is happening, the town Arrernte people – do they go and see the healer, the medicine man? Some go and see the healers that they know. Other healers have started drinking booze, they have frightened away, got rid of, their healing power. People say healers that drink have no power to cure anyone. Their power has been driven away by the booze, and they can't cure anything because their healing power is ruined, destroyed.

The healers that live out bush, their healing powers are still good and healthy. They are the elders, and they still teach the younger people now. But when people sit down near booze, even their children get affected by it. It is a bad influence on the children. When the healers start drinking, they lose their power to cure or to heal. All these things make me sad, but if we can find our way back to how life used to be with our Ancestors and the Land, then maybe our traditional medicines will be all that we need to keep us healthy.

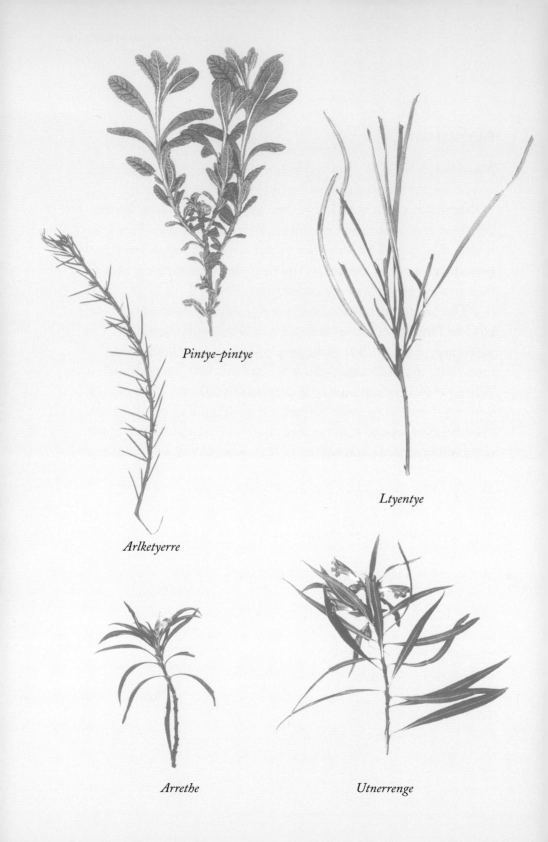

Pintye-pintye

Ltyentye

Arlketyerre

Arrethe

Utnerrenge

APPENDIX

List of plants and insects by common name

common – *Arrernte* – *scientific*

apple bush – pintye-pintye – *Pterocaulon serrulatum*

beefwood tree – *Ityentye* – *Grevillea striata*
bloodwood – arrkernke gum (arrkapere) – *Corymbia opaca*
bush banana, silky pear – atnetye – *Marsdenia australis*
bush fig – utyerrke – *Ficus platypoda*
bush tomato – awele-awele, alperrantyeye – *Solanum ellipticum*

corkwood – untyeye – *Hakea chordophylla*
crimson turkey bush – atnyerlenge – *Eremophila latrobei*

dead finish – arlketyerre – *Acacia tetragonophylla*

emu bush – utnerrenge – *Eremophila longifolia*

ghost gum – arne ilwempe – *Corymbia aparrerinja*

harlequin fuchsia bush – aherre-intenhe – *Eremophila duttonii*

ironwood – athenge, atyarnpe – *Acacia estrophiolata*
itchy grub – ikngenthe – *Ochrogaster contraria*

meat ants – arlkerrke
mulga – arne artetye – *Acacia aneura*

native lemon grass, scented oilgrass – *aherre-aherre* – *Cymbopogon ambiguus*

red poverty bush – *aherre-intenhe* – *Eremophila duttonii*
river red gum bark – *apere* – *Eucalyptus camaldulensis var. obtusa*
rock fuchsia bush – *arrethe* – *Eremophila freelingii*

snake vine – *arratherrke* – *Tinospora smilacina*
striped mint bush – *arrwatnurlke* – *Prostanthera striatiflora*

witchetty bush – *arne atnyeme* – *Acacia kempeana*
white cypress pine, native pine – *irlweke* – *Callitris glaucophylla*

Arne ilwempe

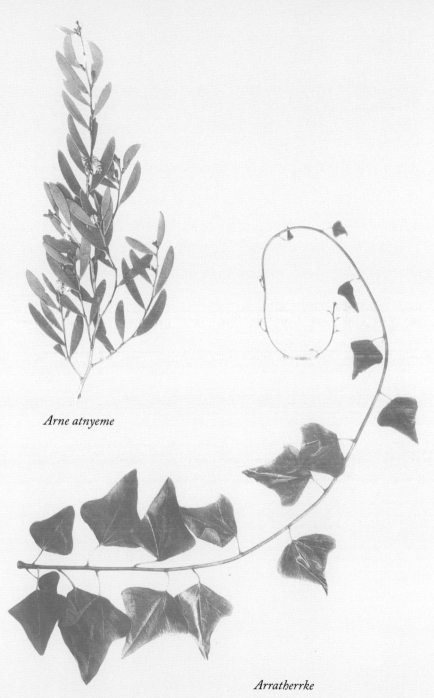

Arne atnyeme

Arratherrke

Index

Bush Foods: Nhenhe-areye anwerne-arle arlkweme: Arrernte foods from Central Australia

MK Turner with John Henderson, illustrated by Shawn Dobson

Shows how Aboriginal people obtain food in an arid environment – from the complex distribution of a kangaroo to the simplicity of enjoying sweet nectar dripping from a corkwood blossom.

ISBN 0 94965 990 8
1994, 80 pp, paperback.
$15.95 S / T

Bushfires & Bushtucker: Aboriginal Plant Use in Central Australia

Peter Latz, illustrated by Jenny Green

Pitjantjatjara, Warlpiri, Arrernte, Pintupi and many other Aboriginal peoples shared their knowledge with Peter Latz to produce this comprehensive account of desert plants. Describes habitat, distribution and use of hundreds of plant species, plus common, scientific and language names.

'without doubt the most authoritative text on the topic'
Malcolm Campbell, ABC

ISBN 0 94965 996 7
416 pp, paperback, line illustrations and colour plates.
$45.00

Anmatyerr Plant Stories: Anmatyerr Ayey Arnang-akert

by the women from Laramba (Napperby) community, compiled by Jenny Green

Provides fascinating insights into the relationship between Aboriginal women and their country. In their own words (with English translations) the Anmatyerr women of Laramba, near Alice Springs, describe their traditions of plant use; includes full-colour photographs of the plants and alphabetical listings and indexes of plant names: Anmatyerr, scientific and common names.

Winner: 2005 MAPDA design award.

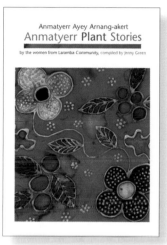

ISBN 1 86465 055 9
2004, 128 pp, paperback, colour.
$24.95

Punu: Yankunytjatjara plant use

compiled and edited by Cliff Goddard & Arpad Kalotas

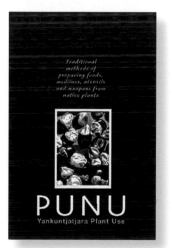

Provides detailed descriptions and illustrations of important plant species that Yankunytjatjara people have used for thousands of years to make food, medicine, utensils and weapons; of great value to anyone interested in the practical uses Aboriginal people make of their environment.

ISBN 1 86465 036 2
2001, 128 pp, paperback.
$24.95